Meet the
TENNESSEE TITANS

BY
ZACK BURGESS

NORWOODHOUSE🏠PRESS

CHICAGO, ILLINOIS

NORWOOD HOUSE 🏠 PRESS

P.O. Box 316598 • Chicago, Illinois 60631
For more information about Norwood House Press please visit our website at
www.norwoodhousepress.com or call 866-565-2900.

Photo Credits:
   All photos courtesy of Associated Press, except for the following: Black Book Archives (6, 7, 15, 18),
   Topps, Inc. (10 both, 11 top & middle, 23), Panini America (11 bottom), Fleer Corp. (22).

   Cover Photo: Mark Zaleski/Associated Press

   The football memorabilia photographed for this book is part of the authors' collection. The collectibles used
   for artistic background purposes in this series were manufactured by many different card companies—
   including Bowman, Donruss, Fleer, Leaf, O-Pee-Chee, Pacific, Panini America, Philadelphia Chewing Gum,
   Pinnacle, Pro Line, Pro Set, Score, Topps, and Upper Deck—as well as several food brands, including
   Crane's, Hostess, Kellogg's, McDonald's and Post.

Designer: Ron Jaffe
Series Editors: Mike Kennedy and Mark Stewart
Project Management: Black Book Partners, LLC.
Editorial Production: Lisa Walsh

LIBRARY OF CONGRESS CATALOGING-IN-PUBLICATION DATA
      Names: Burgess, Zack.
      Title: Meet the Tennessee Titans / by Zack Burgess.
      Description: Chicago, Illinois : Norwood House Press, [2016] | Series: Big
         picture sports | Includes bibliographical references and index. |
         Audience: Grade: K to Grade 3.
      Identifiers: LCCN 2015026327| ISBN 9781599537511 (Library Edition : alk.
         paper) | ISBN 9781603578547 (eBook)
      Subjects: LCSH: Tennessee Titans (Football team)--Miscellanea--Juvenile
         literature.
      Classification: LCC GV956.T45 B87 2016 | DDC 796.332/640976855--dc23
      LC record available at http://lccn.loc.gov/2015026327

288N—072016
Manufactured in the United States of America in North Mankato, Minnesota

CONTENTS

Words in **bold type** are defined on page 24.

The Titans always play with great energy.

Call Me a Titan

In ancient times, people believed in a group of large and powerful gods called "Titans." The Tennessee Titans are large and powerful, too. Their energy on the field sets them apart. Their will to win has produced some of the greatest moments in football history.

TIME MACHINE

The Titans played their first season in 1960, as the Houston Oilers. They were part of the **American Football League (AFL)**. The team moved to Tennessee in 1997 and became theTitans. **Earl Campbell** ●——➤ and Warren Moon were two of the Oilers' biggest stars.

Warren Moon set many team passing records.

There are no bad seats in the Titans' stadium.

Best Seat in the House

The Titans' stadium is located in Nashville, Tennessee. Nashville is nicknamed "Music City." In 1999, the Titans won a game on an amazing play with no time left on the clock. Fans fondly call it the "Music City Miracle."

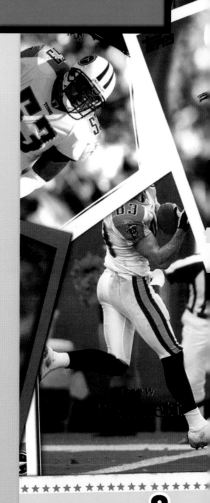

SHOE BOX

The trading cards on these pages show some of the best Titans ever.

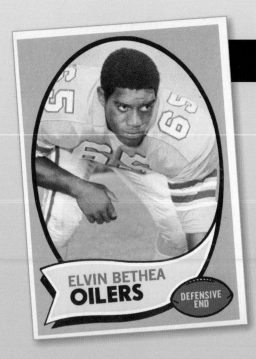

ELVIN BETHEA

DEFENSIVE END · 1968-1983

Elvin was a great pass rusher. He led the team in **quarterback sacks** six times.

EARL CAMPBELL

RUNNING BACK · 1978-1984

Earl crashed into tacklers like a runaway train. He was an **All-Pro** three years in a row.

BRUCE MATTHEWS

OFFENSIVE LINEMAN · 1983-2001

Bruce played 19 seasons with the Oilers and Titans. He was voted into the **Hall of Fame** in 2007.

EDDIE GEORGE

RUNNING BACK · 1996-2003

Eddie was an "iron man" who never got hurt. He reached 10,000 yards for his career in his final game as a Titan.

CHRIS JOHNSON

RUNNING BACK · 2008-2013

Chris was always a threat to score. No one in team history had more touchdown runs of 80 or more yards.

Ken S

11

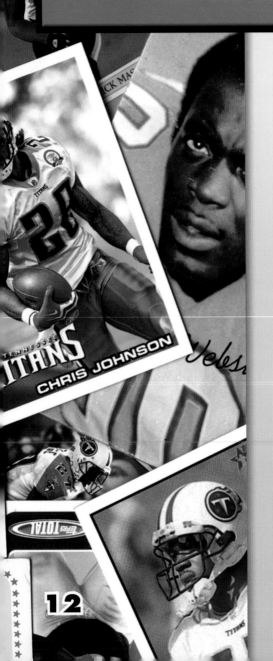

THE BIG PICTURE

Look at the two photos on page 13. Both appear to be the same. But they are not. There are three differences. Can you spot them?

Answers on page 23.

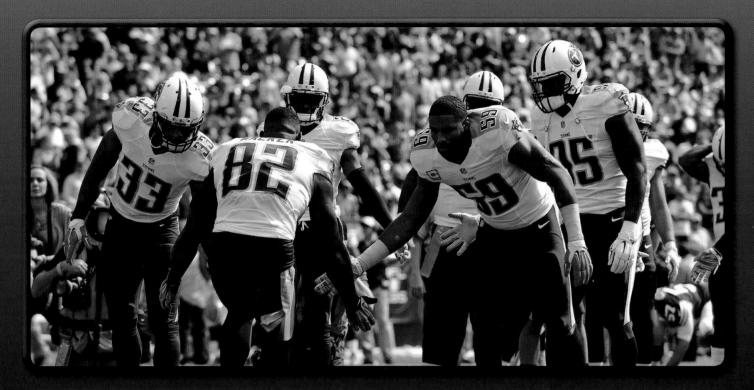

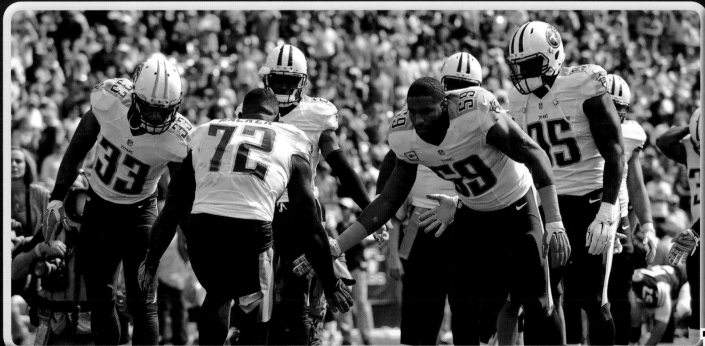

TRUE OR FALSE?

Steve McNair was a star quarterback. Two of these facts about him are **TRUE**. One is **FALSE**. Do you know which is which?

1 Steve was the Most Valuable Player in the National Football League (NFL) in 2003.

2 Steve had to sell his oil wells after the team moved to Tennessee.

3 Steve ran for 36 touchdowns with the Oilers and Titans.

14

Answer on page 23.

Steve McNair was one of the best leaders in team history.

Marcus Mariota signs the shirt of a young fan.

Go Titans, Go!

For every home game, the Titans pick someone to be their "12th Man." It might be a retired player, a celebrity, or one of the team's super fans. They get to plant a sword at midfield to the roar of the crowd.

ON THE MAP

Here is a look at where five Titans were born, along with a fun fact about each.

 WARREN MOON · LOS ANGELES, CALIFORNIA ●————————▶
Warren led the NFL in passing yards in 1990 and 1991.

 DERRICK MASON · DETROIT, MICHIGAN
Derrick caught 453 passes as a Titan.

 MIKE MUNCHAK · SCRANTON, PENNSYLVANIA
Mike played for the team for 12 seasons and then coached the Titans for three years.

 MARCUS MARIOTA · HONOLULU, HAWAII
Marcus threw four touchdown passes in his first NFL game.

 MICHAEL ROOS · TALLINN, ESTONIA
Michael did not miss a single game in his first seven seasons.

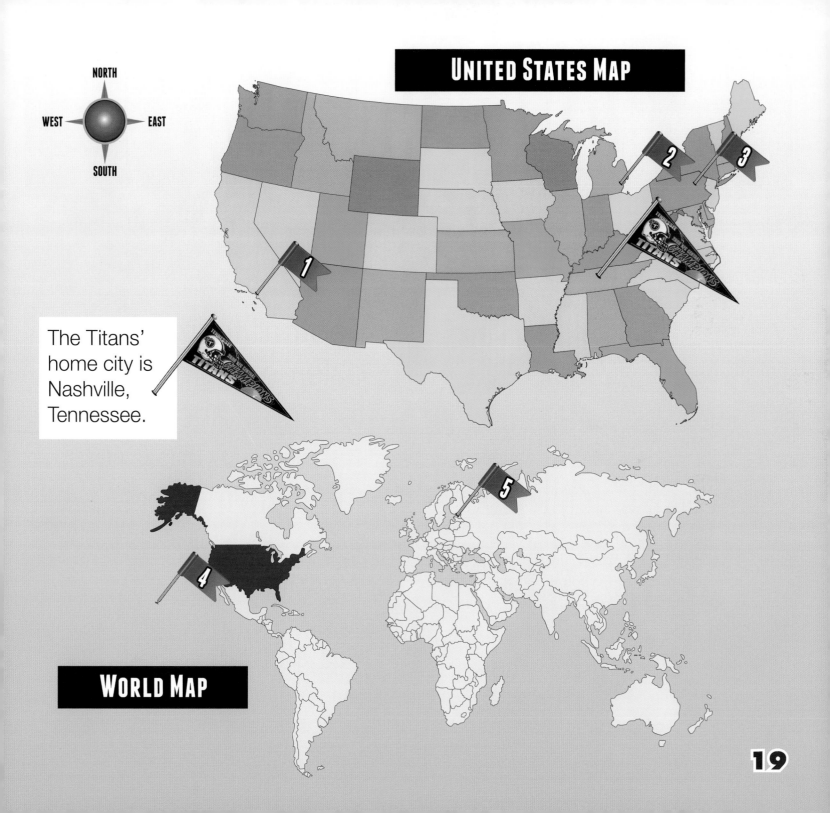

UNITED STATES MAP

NORTH
WEST · EAST
SOUTH

The Titans' home city is Nashville, Tennessee.

WORLD MAP

Marcus Mariota wears the Titans' home uniform.

Football teams wear different uniforms for home and away games. As the Oilers, the team's colors were light blue and white. The Titans added dark blue in 1999.

The Titans' helmet is white with blue stripes down the middle. A circle with the letter *T* appears on each side. Red and blue flames trail behind it.

Delanie Walker wears the Titans' away uniform.

21

The Titans reached the Super Bowl for the first time in 2000. They came within inches of winning the game on the very last play. As the Oilers, the team won a pair of AFL championships. Two of their best players were **Billy Cannon** and George Blanda.

BILLY CANNON
HALFBACK

HOUSTON
OILERS

RECORD BOOK

These Titans set team records.

TOUCHDOWN PASSES	RECORD
Season: **George Blanda** (1961)	36
Career: Warren Moon	196

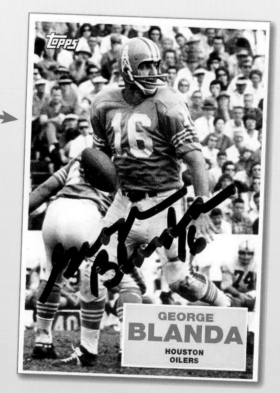

GEORGE **BLANDA**
HOUSTON OILERS

PASS RECEPTIONS	RECORD
Season: Charley Hennigan (1964)	101
Career: Ernest Givins	542

RUSHING YARDS	RECORD
Season: Chris Johnson (2009)	2,006
Career: Eddie George	10,009

ANSWERS FOR THE BIG PICTURE
#82 changed to #72, the stripes on #33's helmet changed to yellow, and #59's wrist bands changed to light blue.

ANSWER FOR TRUE AND FALSE
#2 is false. Steve never owned any oil wells.

Football Words

Index

All-Pro
An honor given to the best NFL player at each position.

American Football League (AFL)
A rival league of the NFL that played from 1960 to 1969.

Hall of Fame
The museum in Canton, Ohio, where football's greatest players are honored.

Quarterback Sacks
Tackles of the quarterback that lose yardage.

About the Author

Zack Burgess has been writing about sports for more than 20 years. He has lived all over the country and interviewed lots of All-Pro football players, including Brett Favre, Eddie George, Jerome Bettis, Shannon Sharpe, and Rich Gannon. Zack was the first African American beat writer to cover Major League Baseball when he worked for the *Kansas City Star*.

About the Titans

Learn more at these websites:
www.titansonline.com • www.profootballhof.com
www.teamspiritextras.com/Overtime/html/titans.html